Psychic Sleuths

Psychic Sleuths

How Psychic Information Is Used to Help Solve Crimes

by

Anita Larsen

An Open Door Book

New Discovery Books
New York

Maxwell Macmillan Canada
Toronto

Maxwell Macmillan International
New York Oxford Singapore Sydney

Cover design by Peg Brier/Studio 27
Book design by Mark David M. Fennell/WRC

New Discovery Books
Macmillan Publishing Company
866 Third Avenue
New York, NY 10022

Maxwell Macmillan Canada, Inc.
1200 Eglinton Avenue East
Suite 200
Don Mills, Ontario M3C 3N1

Macmillan Publishing Company is part of the Maxwell Communication Group of Companies.

First Edition

Printed in the United States of America

10 9 8 7 6 5 4 3 2 1

Library of Congress Cataloging-in-Publication Data
Larsen, Anita.
  Psychic sleuths : how psychic information is used to help solve crimes / by Anita Larsen.
    p. cm.— (An Open Door book)
    Includes bibliographical references and index.
    ISBN 0-02-751645-8   ISBN 0-382-24741-8 PBK
    1. Parapsychology and crime—Case studies—Juvenile literature.
[1. Parapsychology and crime. 2. Extrasensory perception.]
I. Title.
HV8073.5.L37 1994
363.2′52—dc20   93-40593

Summary: A look at the various ways psychics receive information about crimes and the difficulties police face in using psychic information to solve cases. Includes case studies.

Contents

Chapter One
Meet a Psychic Detective

ARE THERE PEOPLE WHO SOMEHOW KNOW things that other people don't? People with psychic abilities?

Nancy Czetli of Greensburg, Pennsylvania, thinks there are.

In fact, Czetli *is* a psychic, but she doesn't think that makes her special. "I don't think psychic ability is any more mysterious than any other talent—writing, painting, skating, or a knack for foreign languages," she said in the April 1, 1992, issue of *Woman's Day*.

Many thousands of people have consulted psychics of one kind or another, asking them personal questions about relationships, health, investments, or career matters. I myself have done so. I kept track of their answers, too. Sometimes those answers turned out to be right; sometimes they didn't. It didn't matter much one way or the other to me; my scorekeeping was all part of the fun of trying to outguess the future.

On a less personal level, I knew that psychics were sometimes consulted to help repair the fabric of society when it was torn by violence or loss. I read about such occasions in newspaper reports of stubborn criminal cases, stories with headlines like POLICE SEARCH RIVER BOTTOM ON PSYCHIC'S SAY-SO. And most of us have seen psychic sleuths on segments of television shows like "Unsolved Mysteries," "20/20," or "Hard Copy." We've watched them on talk shows like "Donahue," "Oprah," and "Geraldo." In fact, the investigative experience some psychic sleuths can claim is more extensive than that of many police officers.

But since no police force had ever called me in to witness how any kind of psychic got his or her investigative information, I myself had no firsthand knowledge of psychic sleuths.

All that changed when a friend decided I should accompany her when she consulted Rebecca Landrum, a channel who lives in Taos, New Mexico. (A channel is someone who allows spirits, or entities, to speak through her or him. Usually, the entity takes over the channel's body after the channel has gone into a trance.) Our purpose in scheduling a session with Landrum was not to gain insight into a criminal case. Instead, we planned to ask questions about personal issues. But before I agreed to ask Landrum those questions, I had some questions to ask *about* Landrum.

I was told that Landrum was unlike some other channels whose names have become almost synonymous with the entity, or being, speaking through them—people like Jane Roberts, who channeled Seth, for example; or J. Z. Knight, who channels Ramtha. Unlike Roberts and Knight, Landrum channels a *group* of entities, who I was assured were gentle and loving, not demonic or evil. This group of beings exists in another dimension from humans, but their primary concern is human spiritual development.

So my friend and I made an appointment.

We pulled into the gravel driveway of a modest Southwestern house. As soon as the car tires stopped crunching over roadbed gravel and the engine was switched off, a couple of sleek, happy-looking cats emerged from the neat rows of a thriving vegetable garden alongside the house. The cats' tails were erect, with the tips bent in the flat crook that usually indicates they're looking forward to something. Considering the time of day, I thought these cats were probably anticipating supper, and I was right.

The cats came to the car to say a polite *purr*, and my friend and I returned the greeting. Everything was feeling so casual and normal that I was beginning to forget what my burning questions for Landrum had been. But that was all right; I'd written them on a yellow legal pad that I clamped under an elbow while I got to know her cats.

Formalities over, the cats went purposefully to the house door, turning to keep an eye on Landrum, a dark-haired woman who had risen from the rows of carrots and was coming from the garden.

"Hi!" she said heartily. "C'mon in."

No "show business" stuff here so far, I noted. The channel was an everyday sort of person, the kind you run into in the grocery store or at the post office or waiting in line at a movie theater.

Inside her home was still more ordinary stuff: papers hanging from refrigerator-door magnets; a small cake pan on the kitchen counter, holding containers of seedlings for the garden; and hungry cats twining around Landrum's legs while she washed garden soil from her hands at the kitchen sink. Everything was almost disappointingly normal, and some of the papers on the refrigerator door—newspaper clippings, wedding announcements, notices of meetings—suggested topics of conversation that were beginning to sound a lot more interesting than my concerns.

But Landrum is a take-charge sort of person. Soon the cats' bowls were filled and the cats were crouching over them, devouring the contents in their daintily demolishing way. We people were firmly adjourned to the living room, where the channeling session would be held.

Once again, the full force of the ordinary hit me. A quilt on the wall and an afghan on the sofa. Some knitting in a basket by one side of an extra-large chair, a tape recorder on a stool on the chair's other side. A framed print of Jesus Christ hung here; metaphysical prints hung there. Two walls of windows, where mini-blinds could only momentarily bar the stream of blazing late-afternoon sunlight. A couple of white candles on one windowsill. All in all, a room in which one would feel comfortable exchanging cookery tips on green-chili stew, which was exactly what we did until Landrum took us in hand.

"Do you have any questions?" she asked me.

"Just these." I took the yellow legal pad from my

lap and got ready to read. I guessed Landrum was ready to hear them. I guessed wrong.

"I mean questions about how this works."

"Oh." I returned the yellow legal pad to my lap and mumbled about having been to psychics before, of course, but never to a channel, so I was . . . well, most interested in . . . Landrum cut me off sternly. I had used the wrong word when I used the word *psychic*.

"Everybody's psychic," she said. "If someone has inner wholeness, then that releases their psychic abilities. But the psychic gift is just a stepping-stone to spiritual growth." She began lighting the candles under one window, and I thought the candles didn't stand much chance of showing up against the sunlight flooding in. She went on, "I channel to help people grow on a soul level. How do I do it?" She was helping me out, asking the questions I'd thought were either silly or insulting. "Some channels are clairvoyant. They see things. Others are clairaudient. They hear. Some are clairsentient. They just *know*. Some channels are all three."

She sat in the big chair, explaining that she mostly heard, as if via crossed telephone wires, remembering what she said later only as she might remember snatches of conversation from a dream.

12

"Channeling is not a logical process, but it can be learned," she said, adding that she went to teachers to learn to channel, then trained herself to hold the energy for longer and longer periods of time. In the beginning of her six years of channeling she could work for only fifteen minutes. Now she was up to around two hours. She approached her work seriously. "This isn't a parlor game," she said.

She cleared her throat. "I'm glad you wrote out your questions. Let's start. You'll catch on."

She settled in comfortably, then commanded, "Breathe!" Her eyes closed, and she began breathing deeply, rhythmically, audibly. So did my friend. So, after a moment, did I.

We all breathed noisily through our noses, and then, shortly, when the room felt dimmer and cooler, Landrum's upper body seemed to be tossed back in her big easy chair. I now understood the reason for the oversized chair that had looked before as if it took up more than its share of space in the room. Her head moved sharply sideways, and she made the sort of sound we might make when someone slaps us or steps unexpectedly and forcefully on our toes. It happened again, and this time both her hands came up, as if to ward off the slapping foot stomper.

Was she all right?

A cat peered around the doorjamb, calmly surveyed the scene, and left. Cat wasn't worried. I glanced at my friend. Still breathing. I forgot about dialing 911 for emergency assistance and went back to breathing myself.

A few minutes later, Landrum's hand shot out to turn on the tape recorder. Then her voice, recognizable but somehow different in its serenity and gentleness, told us we could stop concentrating on breathing. We did. The voice asked if we had any special requests to make. I took advantage of the opportunity to mention some friends who I knew were feeling sad at the moment. The voice told me gently to stop worrying but wouldn't say why, instead asking for my questions. I realized that the entities had registered my concern, and that that was as far as my business in that situation went. My business was *my* business, what I'd come here to ask about.

So I read off my questions, one by one, and listened to the answers. Sometimes I liked what I heard. Sometimes I didn't. Sometimes an answer seemed to be for somebody else's question, one that I hadn't asked.

My friend had told me that might happen, and that if it did, I should rephrase the question. I did. Sometimes I still didn't understand, and that gave the channeled entities a teacherly sort of laugh.

And so it went, through all our questions, until we could see that Landrum was getting tired. She was starting to hug her hands under her upper arms as if her stomach hurt, and dark circles were beginning to shadow her eyes. Later, I learned that Landrum feels dizzy when "they're here and I'm gone."

We thanked the entities and said we were finished. The tape recorder clicked off. The session was over.

But no! The session had suddenly just gone "off the record."

Landrum's finger stabbed at me and her voice told me to take notes, probably because I had a pen and paper. "Sure," I said, flipping over the yellow sheets to get to a clean page.

Almost immediately Landrum's eyes, closed until now, shot open. Then she "went under" again, and this time what my friend and I heard wasn't so pleasant and gentle. This time, we heard from someone not as well put-together, not so focused and channeled as

Landrum's usual group of entities.

Someone, in fact, dead—a murder victim.

Several weeks earlier, the local newspaper had carried the story of a woman, who, along with her seven-year-old son, had been killed on the mesa just outside of town. The two were camping, the article said, and the woman had just finished spreading some clean laundry on bushes to dry overnight when she was attacked by armed killers. When police later found her body, the woman was dead from two gunshots fired at her head. Her son had apparently run from the gunmen, but they'd chased him down and killed him, too. Police found the little boy in the sage a short distance away from his mother, dead like her from two head wounds.

Now Landrum was channeling this dead woman's scattered energy, and it was costing her something. Her hand continually kneaded her forehead, as if she had a pounding headache, and the words tumbled out, ignoring some of the questions my friend and I were able to gather ourselves to put to her, but answering others in a frantic, nervous way.

The woman had some last messages for her family at home. She was intent on those, seeming to have moved beyond anger at her death, past the need to demand justice for her killers. But her spirit was still as shocked and terrified as at the moment of her death, and it showed in how she spoke.

The story of the events of that night emerged brokenly, with many interruptions to stammer out yet another "I'm sorry for leaving you" to her surviving children.

There had been three killers, she said, who came pounding in cowboy boots over the mesa in a drugged haze. The woman had been able to see only one of the men's faces clearly. But she'd heard all of them shouting about their hatred for the hippies who had thronged to the town decades earlier and for Anglos, as white people are called here in New Mexico.

When the woman left, as abruptly as she'd come, her absence was as overwhelming as her presence had been.

Later, when we all had largely recovered from the shocking episode, Landrum said she'd asked her entities to give her information when it was available, to accommodate a friend who had been upset by the murder.

Unbeknownst to any of us, the woman's information had become available the night we happened to be there, and when Landrum's entities left, the woman's energy "simply came and overwhelmed" her. Landrum had sensed it coming for three or four weeks.

Landrum explained that violent deaths often leave victims with "unfinished business" they need to complete. Such business might be emotions victims never took the time to express before, like telling someone how much they loved them, or it might be information the deceased feels compelled to pass along. Tying up these loose ends frees victims to continue their otherworldly journeys without looking back, and such was the case with this woman. Having said finally what she needed and wanted to say, she did not return.

"In a situation like this, I'm just the bridge," Landrum said. "The victims don't know they're gone. They can see what's going on here, but they can't 'get through' to us."

According to Landrum, the next step after a person leaves his or her body is meeting "the guides." These guides aren't anyone the victim knew in life here, and they're not tangible. Therefore the guides are frightening, especially to the victims of violent crimes, who haven't had time to adjust to anything. What needs to happen is for the victims to come to understand that they are no longer living in the same way they were before, when they were "in body," and that the guides are there to help them. When the victims' fears and confusion are released, they can move on.

Usually Landrum doesn't work with crimes like murder. "I know what's coming, so I can 'feel' the murder, and that's very uncomfortable. Sometimes I can actually feel where, say, the bullet went in. It's a dull ache. Also, sometimes psychics have 'known too much,' and they become a suspect."

In 1980, for example, Etta Louise Smith came to the Los Angeles Police Station to report psychic information she'd "seen" about the murder of Melanie Uribe. Uribe was a nurse who'd disappeared on her way to work the night before. She was raped and killed by a blow to the head. Smith reported details that only police had access to. Suspicious authorities threw Smith in jail. Later, after three men were convicted of the crime, Smith sued the city for false arrest, and a jury awarded her $24,184.

Other times, criminals who have a stake in shutting down the flow of information take care to "silence" unwary psychics.

"But maybe the biggest problem in working with murder cases," Landrum said, "is that a psychic can get too involved. Without detachment, there's a big risk of too-great involvement. When you put your psychic gifts into your ego by getting to the place where you *have* to solve a problem, you start to lose your gift because you're taking responsibility for something you don't *own*." A psychic gift is something held only as long as a person works with it, knowing that the gift is granted by a higher power, Landrum believes.

The need of the dead woman we'd heard from that night, like that of many such ghosts, was so strong that she "pushed through" to a channel. That's dangerous because usually the deceased aren't spiritually evolved enough to be aligned to the channel. Landrum's usual group of entities are careful with her, avoiding "power surges."

When Landrum does agree to channel murder-case information, she does so at no charge. "Then it's a service. Or perhaps the interest is karmic," she said. Karma is the force generated by how a person chooses to act in one incarnation, or life, that determines her or his destiny in the next. Karma is a tenet of

Hinduism and Buddhism and is also a belief in many metaphysical religious systems in the Western world.

"We choose our lesson plan before we enter our present lives," Landrum said. "In that sense, predestination operates. But *how* we choose to learn is free will."

My experience at Landrum's channeling session, my only firsthand brush with psychic sleuthing, while unforgettable, was purely accidental. But psychics of one kind or another are often purposively called in by law enforcement officials, by bereaved families, and sometimes, as in cases like random serial killings, by the demands of a terrified public.

In fact, some psychics earn their livings by working with police. Nancy Czetli, for example, has worked on more than 200 homicide cases and has lectured at FBI retraining seminars. Noreen Renier, of Maitland, Florida, has worked as a consultant to law enforcement agencies, including the FBI, throughout the United States and as far away as Japan. There are many others, some of whom you'll meet later in these pages.

In their book *The Blue Sense,* Arthur Lyons and Marcello Truzzi write that psychics should be seen as "extraordinary witnesses," and their work with law enforcement agencies viewed as consulting. Psychics do not claim to solve crimes; police must do that. But psychics can help law enforcement officials by providing what is often a better-than-chance set of directions to follow in solving a crime and piling up evidence that will stand up in court. Dr. Truzzi works with the Psychic Sleuths Project, begun in 1980 at the Center for Scientific Anomalies Research (CSAR) in Ann Arbor, Michigan. The first public report on the information collected so far at the center was published in *The Blue Sense* in 1991.

You'll learn a great deal more about the issues involved in psychic sleuthing in the cases that follow. Perhaps you'll come to decide, as have many supporters of the use of psychics in criminal investigations, that psychics really can help solve crimes and that they are a resource that should be tapped as a matter of course. Or perhaps you'll agree with skeptics who think psychics are bogus—simply "show business" charlatans who interfere with the orderly pursuit of justice.

Chapter Two
Murder, Part I:
The Victim and
a Psychic

WHEN ARE PSYCHICS CALLED INTO A criminal investigation?

Usually when nobody knows what else to do.

Marcello Truzzi's CSAR research shows that most police departments that have used psychics have turned to them only as a last resort.

But sometimes the circumstances at the very beginning of a criminal case indicate that nobody's going to do anything more to solve it than they've already done. Then private people who are deeply involved in the situation, who fear the failure or disinterest of law enforcement officials, and who are, perhaps, seeking to ease the anxiety of inaction or uncertainty, may turn to psychics on their own.

Some or all of these motives were probably operating when Robin Arquette consulted psychic Betty Muench of Albuquerque, New Mexico, on July 22, 1989.

Only days before, three gunshots had been fired from a passing car at Robin's eighteen-year-old sister, Kaitlyn, as she drove home from a Sunday-night dinner at a friend's house. Two of the shots caused grievous, ultimately fatal head wounds.

Later Sunday night, while investigating what they thought was a routine accident on the city's streets—a car had crashed into a telephone pole—Albuquerque police discovered Kaitlyn in that car, still raggedly hanging on to life. Kaitlyn's car had gone out of control after she'd been shot, veering off and slamming into the pole.

Kaitlyn was taken to the emergency room of the University of New Mexico Hospital, and her parents were called. They rushed to the hospital, then relayed the news to Kaitlyn's older brothers and sisters, who came from Florida, Texas, and their own Albuquerque apartments as quickly as they could to join their parents.

Flight difficulties caused Robin, a producer of audio- and videocassettes for children, to be the last of the family to get there in person, but her voice was there almost immediately. Nurses told Kaitlyn's parents that other seriously injured patients had survived, coming out of comas like the one Kaitlyn was in to report knowledge of events that had occurred while they were seemingly completely unaware of anything. A tape of Robin's lullabies, favorites of Kaitlyn's, soon blended with the sound of life-support systems in her hospital room.

Robin arrived the next night, just in time to say good-bye to the little sister she'd been exceptionally close to, even though there was a sixteen-year difference in their ages.

The day of Kaitlyn's funeral, Robin went to the apartment her sister had shared with Dung Nguyen, the boyfriend she'd dated for two sometimes-stormy years. Robin returned to her parents' home, bringing a frilly white dress for Kaitlyn to be buried in, as well as some things from her bedside table. One of those items was a copy of a teenage suspense novel, *Don't Look Behind You,* written by Kaitlyn's mother, writer Lois Duncan.

On July 21, an *Albuquerque Tribune* article covering Kaitlyn's funeral began with the words "Robin Arquette sang her little sister to sleep for the last time Thursday as her friends and family said their farewells." Robin's lullaby tape, which had been played at the hospital, also played at the funeral.

Later that same day, an *Albuquerque Journal*

article followed up on the case from the official point of view. A deputy chief administrative officer for public safety said the general public was not in danger, and Police Chief Sam Baca agreed. "The overall crime rate is down," he said. "Most drive-by shootings are gang related." Earlier media coverage had quoted police calling the shooting a freak accident, a random event.

To Robin and others in Kaitlyn's family, two well-placed gunshots to the head didn't add up to a random accident.

And in addition to having been shattered emotionally by the sudden death of a beloved family member, they were shocked by news about Kaitlyn's boyfriend, Dung, that was coming to light.

Kaitlyn's family had known she planned before her death to ask a girlfriend to move in with her, pushing Dung out. They hadn't known that the apartment manager intended to evict Dung in order to avoid further damage to his premises caused by the young man and his friends. Dung, whom Kaitlyn's family had known as a somewhat shy Vietnamese immigrant struggling to learn American language and customs, was revealed as being so violent that Kaitlyn had once run for safety to her apartment manager.

Kaitlyn's family was also facing some hard truths about Kaitlyn. An honor student in high school and a part-time summer university student while holding down a job at a Pier One store, Kaitlyn had hidden from her family some of her less salutary activities. She had explained to them that Dung survived financially because his aunt in California sent money. "They take care of their own," she'd said. Kaitlyn hadn't told her family what she'd told a friend before her death: she and Dung had been mixed up in a car-wreck scam in California the previous summer, in which insurance payments were collected from the staged wrecks of rental cars.

These bits of information, coming on the heels of numbing grief, increased the family's confusion and pain. And when, soon after Kaitlyn's funeral, Dung was admitted to a hospital because of injuries sustained when he allegedly attempted suicide by stabbing himself in the stomach, their questions mounted even higher.

Would further information make Kaitlyn's death somehow more understandable? the family wondered. They thought that surely police would investigate thoroughly, even though officials seemed to have solved the case to their own satisfaction already.

Troubled, Robin delayed her return flight to Florida. She made an appointment with Betty Muench, a professional channel who uses the technique of automatic writing, a process during which she answers questions by quickly typing out what "comes" or "is given" to her. Robin brought the transcript from this session back to her parents, describing the psychic as "an ordinary woman with an electric typewriter" who didn't charge for working with questions about murders. Not convinced of the value of what they would hear, the Arquettes agreed to listen.

Kaitlyn was angry, the psychic had written. Her anger now was caused by her lack of anger while she was alive. She understood now that her "anger [while] in the body might have saved her anger now." She died because she knew something about a dangerous situation, and she had passed that information along to someone who misinterpreted it to mean that Kaitlyn knew more than she actually did. Earlier the night she was shot, Kaitlyn had done something that endangered her even further. She now knew that she had trusted people whom she shouldn't have trusted.

In spirit, the psychic's report went on, Kaitlyn

remained in a realm where she was still easy to reach. She wanted to communicate because there was much more to be revealed about the situation surrounding her death. Robin had a media contact who would be helpful in this. Robin and Kaitlyn were soul twins, having spent many lifetimes together in lots of different relationships—mother-daughter, best friends, cousins.

Dung had done something that had instigated Kaitlyn's death. Kaitlyn had been trying to urge him to take a certain action, which he had resisted. His friends had encouraged him to resist. He had tried to get Kaitlyn to help him do something, and she had told him he should do something else. He had felt betrayed by Kaitlyn's reaction; Kaitlyn had felt betrayed by his asking. The matter had had to do with right and wrong and also of cross-cultural expectations, but it hadn't been a sufficiently serious matter to have caused what happened.

The report continued, saying that Dung felt remorse about this rather than about some prior argument or disagreement with Kaitlyn. Her death had caused shame and fear in the Vietnamese community. One or two Vietnamese women knew what happened. They had liked Kaitlyn and wanted to come forward, but were afraid to because the men in their lives didn't want them to. Dung knew who shot Kaitlyn.

Kaitlyn's family should take pity on Dung. They should forgive him in her name. The family should not take on the anger and sorrow Kaitlyn felt. Each member of her family would find ways to contact her and help her change her pattern "so that she will be able to release this personality of Kaitlyn and seek to move within the dimension in which she is to reside now." Some on the "other side" would then help her, but before then it would be up to her family to help her, by not giving in to anger and sorrow.

Forgiveness for an unknown wrong that resulted in the death of someone deeply loved is a tall order. But Kaitlyn's father listened to the psychic's report, then phoned the hospital in which Dung was being treated to see if he could have visitors. Dung, in a private room and under surveillance by an Asian orderly, had the right to okay visitors. He didn't want to see Kaitlyn's father, but was eager to see her mother, Lois.

When Robin and her parents went to the hospital, Lois spoke with a heavily sedated Dung. She forgave him for his responsibility in Kaitlyn's death in her daughter's name, and she came away understanding from Dung's words and behavior that he did indeed know something about who shot Kaitlyn, just as the psychic had said. Dung said he would decide about telling police the name of the shooter. When Lois gave this information to detective Steve Gallegos of the Albuquerque Homicide Department, he exclaimed, "That's almost as good as a confession!"

On that seemingly positive note, Robin returned to Florida, and her parents began to attempt to pull their own lives together, convinced that Betty Muench had scored one important "hit" in the first psychic input into this case—Dung knew something.

Then days wore on, bringing what seemed to be no firm official commitment to solving Kaitlyn's murder and piling further confusions on her family. In the face of those confusions, other psychics would be consulted . . . and some disturbing information about her own psychic abilities would be revealed to Kaitlyn's mother.

Chapter Three
Murder, Part II:
The Family and
More Psychics

A MONTH AFTER KAITLYN'S DEATH, HER
parents' lives were settling into a drearily abnormal nor-
mality.

Because she was experiencing blackouts of memory, Kaitlyn's mother began keeping a journal of the
official investigation of her daughter's death and her
reactions to it. Her journal would become *Who Killed
My Daughter?*, a book written to motivate informants
to step forward. She and her husband split what she
called "after-death duties," jobs like disposing of
Kaitlyn's car and clearing her personal effects from her
apartment.

They turned over some letters written in
Vietnamese and postmarked from Orange County,
California, to Detective Gallegos, saying that if the
police couldn't get the letters translated, they'd do it.

No problem, Gallegos said; an officer fluent in
the language was on the force. He added a comment

about his amazement that some people in the department still insisted Kaitlyn's shooting had been random.

"Was it?" Duncan asked.

"Of course not," Gallegos said.

He asked Duncan to question Dung at the police station after he was discharged from the hospital. The interview resulted in a vastly different story from what Dung had said earlier. He now declared he knew nothing about the shooting, and he soon left the city, taken to Kansas City, Missouri, by relatives Kaitlyn's family hadn't known existed.

Lois Duncan also left Albuquerque. She went in order to fulfill a professional commitment she'd made, before Kaitlyn's death, to teach at a writer's conference in Massachusetts. There, at the end of a drive through dense fog on unfamiliar roads, she found a confusion over check-in time and hotel-room keys. That night she ended up sleeping in a porch chair overlooking the marshes at the edge of Cape Cod and reading a book a friend back home had handed to her.

The book was written by a psychotherapist, and it dealt with his experiences with a patient who recalled past lives. Part of the book described the stages of spiritual existence that separated the patient's incarnations.

The book reaffirmed Betty Muench's information about the current whereabouts of Kaitlyn's spirit.

Early the next morning, Duncan returned a phone call from one of her sons in Albuquerque. His news, delivered in tones of happy elation, was that he'd seen Kaitlyn. Not dreamed about her, but seen her. And she was doing all right.

This was the first family member to make contact with Kaitlyn; others would later check in with her parents to report similar experiences of epiphany, just as Muench had said they would.

Duncan returned home from her teaching stint to face an agony of loss, haunting Kaitlyn's grave between bouts of "after-death duties." Then a new clue surfaced in Kaitlyn's forwarded mail.

A telephone bill listed charges for a series of brief telephone calls made from Kaitlyn's apartment placed only minutes after her death. At that time Dung was in the hospital with the family, and no one was supposed to have been in the apartment. Who had called? And why?

The bill set forth these mysteries and at the same time provided solid clues to its resolution—numbers whose owners could be identified. This and other new information led Duncan to phone Robin, who worked in a credit bureau to support her fledgling recording business. Robin said she'd check the telephone numbers . . . if her mother would make an appointment with Betty Muench.

Duncan resisted. "In the beginning, I didn't believe in it at all," she says. Still, Robin's information from her session with Muench had been eye-opening. She made an appointment and went, stopping at a church on the way to pray for guidance.

Muench told Duncan she rarely worked on crime cases. "The Albuquerque police won't accept information from psychics, and it's infuriating when they refuse to follow up on leads," she said. The anger that usually came from crime victims was an additional depressing factor. But since she'd gotten involved in Kaitlyn's death through Robin, Muench felt obligated to continue, which she did at no charge.

Duncan waited in Muench's small book-lined home office as Muench sat at her electric typewriter and took some long, slow breaths. Finally Muench said she was ready. "It seems to work best to start off by asking the deceased how she is and if she has a message for you," she said. "After that you can ask her about specifics."

Duncan did so. "The Deity seems to be encouraging her to respond," Muench said after some preliminary, focusing remarks. "That's pretty unusual. Have you been praying about this?"

What Duncan gained in this and later sessions led her to say in a conversation we had about her experiences, "I believed in Betty totally." Muench's obvious sincerity and the speed at which she typed, a speed that allowed no time for composition, convinced a professional writer that Muench wasn't making things up. But at the same time, Duncan inserted a caveat: She believed in Betty, rather than in her information.

That information included the prospect that when Duncan got her emotional act together and Kaitlyn learned to transmit better, they wouldn't need a psychic go-between. She also said that the killing shots came from a low-rider car like those often driven by Hispanic kids in the area. On an ominous note, Muench added that before this was over, someone else might be killed.

In that first session, Muench also "read" some objects that had belonged to Kaitlyn by handling them, a psychic skill called psychometry. She said that Kaitlyn had seen the shooter—and recognized him. She had constantly checked her wristwatch with a 9:00 P.M. time in mind throughout the evening before she was shot, and she sensed some kind of setup. She was surprised when she was overtaken by the low-rider, expecting the person she recognized to be somewhere else. Also, Kaitlyn visited someone that evening who didn't want to see her, someone who had, in effect, slammed the door in her face.

Several days later, Duncan heard from police that they had received a letter from an anonymous informant. The letter said that Kaitlyn had known the person who shot her, and that he had fired from a low-rider car.

When Muench's information was proven right again, Duncan's attitude toward psychics began to soften. Now, she told me, she would "ask when there was something specific she needed to know in order to help her take the right action." She would take the information and run with it because she felt sure that Kaitlyn's messages were being relayed, through her spiritual "guides," to Muench.

Thanksgiving arrived, and then Christmas. Family traditions were broken by Kaitlyn's absence. Robin, home for the holidays, helped Duncan staple posters around the city offering a reward for information about the case. Some people didn't want them to do that. One car gave them a dangerous high-speed "escort" from a neighborhood, and after that, when Duncan stapled up posters, she made sure that there was a nearby exit when she stopped. She also began interviewing Kaitlyn's friends, searching for any bit of information that might contradict the police theory of a random drive-by shooting.

Then, on January 19, 1990, the *Albuquerque Journal* ran a story that seemed to prove the random-shooting theory unquestionably. Police had found an eyewitness to the shooting and arrested three young Hispanic men who were involved. The story's headline read, TEEN SHOT AT YOUNG WOMAN ON A DARE, OFFICERS SAY.

Miguel Garcia was the shooter, and the others arrested were Dennis (Marty) Martinez and Juvenal (Juve) Escobedo, a Mexican national. They'd been driving a low-rider, a Camaro. The witness was Robert Garcia, a backseat passenger who had simply been with the three suspects on a joyride and was not charged.

These events sparked a campaign of telephone death threats to Duncan and her husband that frightened them into hiding. Their move was an eerie echo of the plot of Duncan's novel *Don't Look Behind You*, which centered on a family forced into hiding as relocated witnesses for the FBI. Relocated witnesses are those who have given authorities information that endangers them and their family. In return, the family is helped to adopt a new—and what is hoped to be safer—name, history, and residence.

By the end of January, murder charges against two of the suspects were dropped. Police had pressured Robert Garcia into making his "eyewitness" statement. The headline of a story written by Mike Gallagher, investigative reporter, read TEEN SAYS HE LIED TO POLICE ABOUT SEEING ARQUETTE SHOOTING. Because there is a limitation on the length of time suspects can be held without being indicted by a grand jury, police withdrew the murder charges, intending to reissue them later, after gathering more evidence. They filed unrelated charges of burglary against Miguel Garcia to keep him in jail and released the other two men on bail.

The random-shooting theory held by the police

seemed to have unraveled completely, but several days later a police sergeant told Duncan, "You're simply going to have to face up to the fact that your daughter died because she was in the wrong place at the wrong time."

On January 29, 1990, the day *before* the newspaper ran the story about the police pressure that led to the dropping of the murder charges, Duncan had called Muench for another reading. Before the appointment, Muench called back to say there was no need for Duncan to come in. She'd had some spare time to work on the case and could report what she'd gotten now, over the phone.

What she'd "gotten" was Kaitlyn's insistence on the initials *R & J*, written exactly that way. It was seemingly the name of a business, since Muench had seen it written on the door of a white vehicle. Muench said that turning over all the information Duncan had gathered to reporter Mike Gallagher would be a good way to keep the case alive. In her trance, Muench had perceived him as a "great bomb," a media person who would seem to drop out of the case but would continue working undercover to see it to its resolution.

In a public library, Duncan found phone books

for Orange County, California, the location of the rental-car-wreck insurance scam Dung and Kaitlyn had been involved in. She discovered a phone listing for R & J. Checking that led her to the knowledge that the firm's phones had been disconnected about the same time Kaitlyn was shot.

A master of fictional plotting, Duncan applied her skills to this new information. She turned over in her mind the idea that the Hispanics could have been gunmen hired by the Vietnamese. This notion could breathe fresh life into the criminal investigation. But the real excitement of Betty Muench's R & J reading was Duncan's shock of recognition that Kaitlyn was indeed still there—and communicating valuable information!

Subsequent events added fresh hope that Kaitlyn's killers would be found. Reporter Mike Gallagher was turning up new information about Dung's role in the shooting. Dung's name had been tied into the drug-dealing street scene. And when Miguel Garcia was arraigned on the burglary charges, the judge gave the state a deadline to indict him for Kaitlyn's murder, so police rushed their case to the grand jury.

A grand jury indictment would mean there was enough evidence to continue investigating the case. The grand jury indicted both Miguel Garcia and Juve Escobedo, handing down warrants for their arrests. By this time, Escobedo had skipped bail and apparently left the city.

A spring 1990 reading by Betty Muench elicited the information that the shooting had been a smooth operation. A symbol like a snake appeared. Muench said this symbol was tied to some "great clan or force, and this will have power and wealth, and there will be the hiring of what they consider lesser ones—the Hispanics." A Vietnamese "snake" used Hispanics to do his dirty work, then threw them away, Muench explained. (Three-plus years later, California investigators told Duncan that Asian smugglers of drugs and illegal immigrants are known as "snake heads.") Miguel Garcia had sought the "honor" of being the shooter, and he thought he was being protected by the "snake," but he wasn't. Added to this was the pressure of the possibility that the police would find the missing Escobedo and "cut a deal" with him that would leave Garcia standing alone.

Duncan's husband thought they should share this reading with newsman Gallagher, since the police no longer answered their questions or shared information with them. Even the Vietnamese letters turned over to the police in the days after Kaitlyn's death seemed to have disappeared! But Gallagher wasn't receptive to psychic information.

By this point Duncan had accepted that it was possible for a medium to channel information from the dead. But how could anyone foretell the future? Her husband suggested she think in terms of a videotape created in a realm where time as we know it doesn't exist, where things aren't bracketed by beginnings and endings, where—as Landrum had put it—free will could be applied to an overall predestined script. Psychics like Betty Muench, Duncan's scientist husband said, could have the ability to zero in on the videotape of a person's life at any point, even before the events on it took place in our reality.

If that was so, it led to a chilling possibility for Duncan. A person in a creative career, like a writer, continually draws on information stored in the depths of the subconscious. Could she have pulled up fragments from scenes on a videotape that hadn't yet been played out when she wrote?

Strange coincidences from Duncan's work and life seemed to suggest that. In *Don't Look Behind You,* for example, Duncan had modeled her heroine, April, on her daughter Kaitlyn's personality. In the story April was chased by a hitman in a Camaro, and that had happened to Kaitlyn a month after the book came out. And in the book April's family was forced into hiding to avoid violence from a ruthless drug ring. Kaitlyn's family had also been forced into hiding, but so far little evidence of an organized drug ring had entered the case.

Duncan read through the entire police case file again in early fall. She found the transcript of an interview held by Detective A. V. Romero with Robert Garcia, the "eyewitness" pressured by police into saying he'd been with the other men the night Kaitlyn was shot. Robert Garcia said that Miguel Garcia was called Mike, and that his nickname was Vamp. Duncan had not only given the hitman in *Don't Look Behind You* a Camaro to drive, but she had also named him Mike Vamp!

At the end of August, Mike Gallagher mailed Duncan a copy of an interview former ally Detective Gallegos conducted with Dung on July 9, 1990. He included a note saying that after the tape recorder was turned off and the interviewer went "off the record,"

Gallegos told Dung that he had grounds for a libel suit against Kaitlyn's parents because of the things they'd suggested were true about him.

Inconsistencies in Dung's story in this interview were not followed up by police, and if there was a Vietnamese-speaking police officer in the Albuquerque police force, she or he had not been invited to help conduct the interview. Dung sounded completely ill at ease in the English language, coming off as a "poor soul" being badgered by Kaitlyn's family.

When Duncan herself followed up the inconsistencies in this interview, she became even more convinced of Vietnamese involvement in her daughter's death. But the new information she found could not be used in the courtroom by the prosecution unless it was presented by the police, and that seemed a very remote possibility, given the family's current relationship with authorities.

Attempting to sort all this out, Duncan got in touch with Marcello Truzzi, an old high-school friend, now head of the Psychic Sleuths Project at the Center for Scientific Anomalies Research. Perhaps his work with CSAR would enable him to provide insights into how psychics could work with police. She also wrote to

Dr. William Roll, project director for the Psychical Research Foundation, an institute that serves as a scientific and educational research center to investigate the possibility of the life of the consciousness after the death of the physical body. Maybe Roll could provide backup for the information Betty Muench was getting from Kaitlyn, as well as offer some answers about the disturbing correlation between Duncan's novels and her life. For a related writing job, Duncan also wrote letters to psychics Noreen Renier, Greta Alexander, and Nancy Czetli, all of whom had worked in criminal investigations.

The first psychic to answer Duncan's letter was Noreen Renier, who usually worked with police on crimes because they were in a position to follow up clues. As a police aid, Renier typically held two sessions per case. In the first, she described the criminal to a police artist, who made a sketch of the face. In the second, she tried to enter the mind of the killer.

Renier's response focused on the personal tragedy Duncan and her husband had suffered. Duncan followed up by telephone, and Renier offered to "get a face" from objects Kaitlyn had worn. "I charge the police for my work, but I'll do this for you for free,"

Renier said. Duncan immediately sent some of Kaitlyn's belongings, including her watch and the earrings she'd been wearing when she was shot. She also made arrangements to send the cross Kaitlyn had worn, which had been given to a favorite cousin.

Renier worked with an assistant who asked questions while she was in a trance, and the session was audiotaped. She offered to do a phone hookup so that Duncan could be "on the scene"; she would also be sending along the tape and the artist's drawing.

The phone hookup didn't work. Duncan was too attached to the case and too emotional about it. Her thoughts interfered with what Renier could get from Kaitlyn. They hung up, and for the next two hours, Duncan sat by the telephone, waiting for a return call and "sending messages" to Kaitlyn: *Take advantage of this opportunity to get a message to us. Send us more than a picture of Miguel Garcia.*

Finally Renier called back to say that she'd mail what she'd gotten. Three days later Duncan received the police-artist sketches of Kaitlyn's killers and Renier's audiotape.

There were two sketches. The first looked hazily familiar to Duncan, as if it were a newspaper photograph she'd seen before. The second sketch was a knee-buckler. Kaitlyn hadn't sent a message to Renier showing alleged Albuquerque shooter Miguel Garcia, called Mike and Vamp. She'd done something even more important, something privately symbolic.

The second sketch showed the fictional Mike Vamp, the interstate drug-ring hitman shown on the cover of the *British* edition of *Don't Look Behind You,* a face few people in the United States other than Kaitlyn had seen! Certainly Noreen Renier had not seen this edition of the book. Dr. Roll later explained this phenomenon as "displacement." "Instead of hitting the target you hit somewhere around the target. . . . The drug connection is the significant thing."

Renier's audiotape was also a surprise. She didn't place Kaitlyn at her friend's house all evening for a quiet Sunday-night dinner the night she was shot. Renier said Kaitlyn had been somewhere else, a place at which she was threatened with a knife. Renier recommended that Kaitlyn's family get in touch with the Albuquerque police or the FBI, but Duncan said they'd tried these avenues of investigation and had been stymied by both.

Renier pointed out that she'd done what she could do. "Psychic detective work is based on impressions. The case is a jigsaw puzzle—you get a lot of pieces and you know they'll make a picture—but putting it all together is a job for the police," she said.

Duncan returned to her copy of the police-department file, only to discover that different witnesses had offered evidence that there was in fact a disparity between Kaitlyn's known movements on the night she was shot and the time that actually elapsed. She hadn't gone straight from her parents' home to her friend's. Three hours were unaccounted for. Duncan asked Renier to look at those hours, and Renier did.

On the night she was shot, Renier's mailed report of this session said, Kaitlyn left her parents' home to go to the parking lot of a shopping mall, where she'd met an old boyfriend. From the mall, she'd gone to a "desert castle," a house somewhere in the heights of Albuquerque, where she saw somebody politically important buying cocaine. Her seeing this was met with anger, and she was turned away. From the "desert castle," she'd gone tearfully to her friend's house for dinner, checking her wristwatch and crying often. From her friend's home, she'd begun to drive to her parents' home, but was cut off by people sent from "the hill." Those people killed her execution-style—two shots were fired to the head.

"The crime that was committed against me," said Renier, speaking as Kaitlyn, "was to silence me. *I will never be silenced!*" When Renier-as-Kaitlyn was asked if Kaitlyn had anything to tell her mother that she hadn't told before, Kaitlyn said, "Don't stop what you're doing. Just remember the police have fear. These are very powerful people who are involved. The police are frightened. . . . They want to mark it up as something different than it is and not to go beyond that." Kaitlyn insisted she'd been shot because of the drug transaction of the important person she'd seen.

Later, Nancy Czetli responded to Duncan's letter. She also agreed to do a reading. Czetli wanted no information at all except crime-scene videotape footage. From news-broadcast videocassettes of Kaitlyn's car and the telephone pole it had hit, Nancy Czetli "got" money changing hands at Kaitlyn's death. She saw grief in Dung, but also a sense of his anger, and satisfaction that Kaitlyn had finally been "put in her place" according to Vietnamese gender roles.

The Hispanics, Czetli said, did the shooting after checking Kaitlyn's license plate against a number written on a piece of paper. Kaitlyn had been followed and chased. With a more powerful car, she might have gotten away. Kaitlyn was a nice girl, but she'd been naive and had gotten caught up in something bigger than she was, something fueled by drug money. The Hispanics, known for random violence, had been hired by the drug bosses. Kaitlyn had experienced threats of violence from a Vietnamese knife.

"I don't have much hope about the trial of Garcia," Czetli said. "It's my feeling that this was set up with Hispanic hitmen, because if any Oriental person had been seen around her with a gun, the whole mess would have come out immediately. So they used a completely different racial setup to distract.

"But," she added, "they *did* have some kind of connection. And I don't know if it was the boyfriend himself or through his network, but I feel that they had a connection to Hispanic hitmen. Within a drug network you can ask people to do things."

Duncan asked how Czetli had gotten such precise information.

"I work best from the crime scene itself," Czetli replied. Frightened people leak information mentally, she said, and "somehow it gets stuck in the cells of the environment. I don't understand exactly how it works, except that I know that cells can, in fact, store information. . . . They reflect scars from the scenery that stay a long time."

Czetli also said she saw the thought pattern from the murder scene through Miguel Garcia's eyes. That pattern was repeated in the news footage of courtroom scenes in which she could see Garcia's eyes. "From the time I locked eyes with Garcia, I was sure they had the right person," she said.

Czetli's reading ended with these words: "I hope you know that your daughter has an existence now. . . . Her soul has an awareness of how much you care . . . and when you think loudly about her she is very much aware of what you're thinking. I get the distinct impression that she is trying very hard to communicate with you through dreams and even directly. She's trying to make you feel and realize that her soul has continued." She repeated that Kaitlyn had been naive and had acted rashly—and added that everything that happened was her choice.

The family's second Christmas without Kaitlyn was approaching. Information from Renier and Czetli was so similar that after six months of silence Duncan contacted Muench again to see if she had any further news. Muench added to the record the news that Kaitlyn had returned to her apartment the night she was shot. Then her report echoed those of the other psychics: Kaitlyn went on from her apartment to the "desert castle," where she saw a drug transaction in which an "urgent" buy was made by a powerful man.

In a later session, Czetli said that Kaitlyn was having difficulty sending messages because she herself was so urgent and eager to communicate. And at the end of February 1991, Greta Alexander checked in by phone after midnight to say that "there's more to Kaitlyn's death than meets the eye"; her boyfriend had had something to do with it, and he was involved in unethical situations. Kaitlyn was still uneasy, Alexander said, but she hadn't been killed in order to silence her. She'd been shot because somebody had been using her, and the whole situation snowballed.

Over the next year, Duncan did some library research on the drug trade and discovered a vital connection among Albuquerque, El Paso, and Los Angeles. Then, in the spring of 1992, newspaper reports on the case began to appear again. An *Albuquerque Tribune* article of April 24, 1992, was headlined POLICE BLAST-

ED ON ARQUETTE CASE. A *Journal* article of that day was headlined DA DROPS CHARGES IN ARQUETTE SHOOTING and reported the release of Miguel Garcia. The next day, a *Tribune* headline read FORMER SUSPECTS STILL UNDER SCRUTINY IN ARQUETTE SLAYING, and the article acknowledged a possible connection to Vietnamese gang activity, as well as a possible connection to the narcotics trade.

It appears that the psychics were ahead of the police at every step of this criminal investigation, so an unpublished March 1992 Muench reading that Duncan shared with me is especially interesting in light of the articles that appeared a month later.

There had been much energy expended on Kaitlyn, Muench said, and it would result in a "collar on the wolf." Kaitlyn now "leans back in satisfaction. There is much warmth and softness in her now." But the "wild wolf has something on its neck as it howls, its neck up in the air."

Chapter Four
Police and Psychics

IF THE PSYCHICS WORKING ON THE KAITLYN Arquette case were so solidly in agreement about the facts behind her killing, why did the Albuquerque police department and the FBI hesitate to accept their information?

Undoubtedly there are reasons specific to this case, but there are some general reasons why police back away from psychics.

One is the way psychics talk. As Dr. Roll says, psychics "get impressions rather than absolutes." They provide guidelines rather than facts. An example of this is Noreen Renier's "displaced" description of Kaitlyn Arquette's killer that resulted in the police artist drawing the face of a British illustrator's depiction of Kaitlyn's mother's fictional hitman Mike Vamp, rather than the alleged real-life hitman Miguel Garcia, nicknamed Mike and Vamp.

This clue was a "private" clue. It needed to be

interpreted with the sensitivity Duncan showed when she said it was symbolic, and that what Kaitlyn was communicating was the connection of her death to the working pattern of an interstate drug ring. Fitting this clue into the loop of an official investigation would have been difficult, if not impossible, because those outside the communications system of Duncan's family wouldn't have access to the symbolic information needed to do that.

Information from psychics needs a good interpreter. Dorothy Allison, a psychic who worked with Des Plaines, Illinois, police on the 1978 serial-killings case that resulted in the conviction of John Wayne Gacy, has found a couple of good police interpreters. Detective Sal Lubertazzi, her former sidekick and interpreter, says, "Dorothy sees things, but she doesn't know geographical locations. Sometimes she'll say you have to go south [to find a body]. If you do, and we don't find anything, I'll tell the police department to go north. It's kind of hard to explain." Baltimore detective Al Darden, who has also worked with Allison, says, "I didn't know how to work with her then, but I do now. She might give you number seventy-one, for example. In reality, it might be seventeen. You have to make facts out of what she says."

Sometimes an interpreter has to make sense out of a psychic's actual words as well as out of the facts they convey. Channeler Rebecca Landrum uses the word *channelese* to describe the sometimes impenetrable language of what she receives from her group of entities. The communications often come in what is almost a foreign language because it is so full of outdated words or highly formal usage. It's easy to stumble over both kinds of expressions.

Betty Muench's January 29, 1990, reading for Lois Duncan is an example of this. The reading begins, "There is an image of a flat bed with a great bomb on it. It will be that this will be for show and that there will be many other weapons that will be available in this. There will be this which will show that by putting this into the hands of the media there will be this which will not be allowed to become buried and intimidated." While some readers will receive a clear message from this, others are likely to respond with confused frustration.

Many psychics say the difference between ordinary talk and channelese arises because they are working from the right side of their brains. Current biological theories say the right hemisphere of the brain controls creativity, intuition, and pattern recognition. The left hemisphere of the brain is the analytic, logical side. When the symbolic, right-brain language of psychics is overlaid on rational expectations, what results can sound silly. And it works the other way, too. "Silliness" can result when a good critic writes overanalytically about a great painting, a great meal, a great wine, or great music.

Individual police officers may have a "blue sense" that's more right-brain than left-brain. "Blue sense" is a heightened intuition of events that is based on a bit more than experience. An officer with "blue sense" may have a hunch that a car turning down a dark alleyway between shops is up to no good. So she follows the car and is able to arrest a burglar caught in the act. The hunch that motivated the officer's behavior may be connected with her rational knowledge of a rash of burglaries in the neighborhood or in shops similar to those reached via the alley. But why *that* car? *That* alleyway? *That* night? The officer with "blue sense" probably won't be able to answer specifically and factually.

As a group, however, police forces are among the most conservative of social institutions. Oftentimes the need to resort to a psychic embarrasses them and the investigative methodology they've been trained to use. So many police departments appear skeptical of psychic information. They think that psychic "leads" in a case can call for too many more police work hours and tax dollars to follow up on than the leads prove to be worth in the end. Also, police often feel that psychics lend a circuslike atmosphere to a serious investigation.

The basis of our judicial system is another stumbling block to official acceptance of information gained psychically. The American criminal-justice system is based on the assumption of innocence until proven guilty. The role of police in our system is to find the facts that a prosecuting attorney can then place before a judge and jury. A psychic's "knowledge" is not admissible as evidence in a court of law, so police can't rely on psychics when they're building a case against an alleged criminal.

There's another twist in that knot for police: probable cause. Police have to have good reasons— probable cause—to arrest suspects. If they don't, a competent defense attorney can work that lack to his or her client's advantage in order to reduce the sentence or even to get the case thrown out of court.

"Say a psychic with a good track record gives detectives detailed clues in a murder case," write the authors of *The Blue Sense*, "including the name and address of a suspect. On the basis of that, police search the man's house and find a knife with blood on it that matches the blood of the victim. In addition, they find a pair of shoes with mud on the soles that places the man at the location where the victim's body was found. The suspect is arrested and confesses, but as the arrest was illegal because of a lack of probable cause, none of the evidence—the knife, the shoes, et cetera—can be used."

Probable cause led to a legal challenge of the outcome of a Chicago trial in 1978. In this case, hospital worker Allen Showery confessed to the murder of nurse Teresita Basa after detectives told him that Basa had accused him. Her accusation was channeled through the body of a mutual acquaintance of theirs, Mrs. Remibias Chua. Chua had been in a trance, and the "voice" had spoken in Tagalog, the native Philippine language of both Chua and Basa.

When Chua and her husband contacted police with this information, it came at a propitious time. Police were months into their investigation of Basa's murder. Detectives had run out their leads, and further search was stalled. Showery denied guilt when he was questioned. But when told that the "voice" said the woman he was living with had a ring that had belonged to the dead woman, Showery broke down. He confessed that he'd killed Basa and stolen her ring.

During the trial, Showery's attorney tried to have the case dismissed on the grounds that a voice from the grave was not probable cause for an arrest. But the judge ruled that Showery had spoken voluntarily to the detectives and that he hadn't been arrested until after his confession.

The defense motion for dismissal was denied *and* Mrs. Chua's psychic revelations were admitted into testimony in this case, but Chua's information shocked the jurors. One or two jurors laughed, some put their heads in their hands, and one stood up in disgust. The disclosure that a psychic had helped with the investigation resulted in a hung jury, and Showery wound up receiving a minimum fourteen-year sentence as part of a plea-bargaining deal.

Despite the possibility of challenges like this one, many police departments appear to be changing their minds about the usefulness of psychic sleuths. A 1979 survey conducted by the California Department of Justice concluded that "a talented psychic can assist you by helping to locate a geographic area of a missing person, narrow the number of leads to be concentrated upon, highlight information that has been overlooked, or provide information previously unknown to the investigator."

And the Pomona Police Department in California has even written official policy for the use of psychic sleuths. Lieutenant Kurt Longfellow wrote the policy under the guidance of Dr. Louise Ludwig, a psychologist and psychic researcher. Ludwig founded PsiCom, a group of five college professors and administrators that was active from the late 1970s through the middle 1980s. PsiCom, no longer in existence, was a "professional behavioral science organization seeking to provide service to law enforcement personnel seeking new investigative techniques." In 1989, Lieutenant Longfellow said his police department had "come out of the closet," and that "even though they'll never admit it, LAPD has been using psychics for years."

Also in 1989, Des Plaines, Illinois, chief of police Joseph Kozenczak wrote an article for *Policing* magazine, an influential periodical in the field, in which he said he thought police should consult psychics on a regular basis: "Rather than as a last resort, psychics could be helpful on a more practical basis."

In 1986, several scientists at the FBI's Behavioral Science Unit in Quantico, Virginia, took a courtroom stand supporting a psychic with whom they'd worked. They testified on behalf of psychic Noreen Renier in a libel suit she brought against writer John Merrell, who had written an article in which he said Renier was a fraud. But the scientists confirmed that Renier had done unofficial assessments for the FBI and that she had, as she contended, predicted (during a lecture at the FBI Academy in January 1981) the attempted assassination of President Reagan. The jury was convinced by the scientists' testimony; they awarded Renier $25,000 from Merrell.

Law enforcement agencies appear now to be echoing the feelings of many private citizens about the positive worth of psychic information. A 1990 Gallup Poll found that 49 percent of all Americans believed in extrasensory perception. Another 22 percent weren't sure about it, and 14 percent had themselves consulted a fortune-teller or psychic.

Skeptics argue that even when a psychic has sued

for false arrest and won (as did Etta Louise Smith, whose psychic information about the murdered Melanie Uribe landed her in jail, and whose later suit against the city of Los Angeles led a jury to hand her a little more than $24,000), nothing has been proved except perhaps that the police acted improperly. These skeptics have a point: Because someone wins a suit for false arrest, that doesn't prove that they're psychic.

But skeptics who demand "proof" of specific cases where information provided by a psychic has resulted in convictions gain little support for their stance even if they find "proof" or "disproof" of the psychic's role in a specific case. Even arrest and extensive prosecution of a suspect may not lead to conviction, for many reasons that have nothing to do with the psychic's role. The authors of *The Blue Sense* feel that the data available at present can't arrive at the kind of "scientific" proof the skeptics want. That kind of proof can only come from a comparison of conviction rates of cases that used psychics with those that didn't. That information simply isn't available.

The most vocal skeptics are groups like the Committee for the Scientific Investigation of Claims of the Paranormal, or CSICOP. This group, headquartered in Buffalo, New York, held a press conference on December 10, 1982, during which its representatives blasted police departments for their use of psychic detectives. The CSICOP chairman, Professor Paul Kurtz, was quoted in the press release as saying that "there is no hard data that self-proclaimed psychics have been able to help detectives in unearthing criminals or lost persons."

Later, a spokesman for an offshoot of CSICOP was concerned about how often psychics misidentify persons as murderers and damage innocent people's reputations. He offered no specific evidence to support his charge, nor did he give any comparison rates for miscarriages of justice that resulted from conventional police practices.

The CSICOP position was summed up in its 1982 press release: "Calling in the occult to assist in what should be serious, important work is a step back into the Middle Ages, and is dismaying to witness in today's enlightened world." Some religious fundamentalist groups would heartily agree with both the tone and the content of this statement, and so would some traditional scientists.

Whereas neither side of this issue can either

prove or disprove its position, a few surveys have been conducted to determine how widespread police use of psychics actually is. Many, if not most, police forces said they have received unsolicited psychic information, but all the surveys conclude that psychics haven't been used effectively all that often. Dr. Martin Reiser, head of the Los Angeles Police Department's Behavioral Sciences Service Section, said in a 1989 interview with Marcello Truzzi, "We continue to get anecdotal reports, but no additional data has emerged to suggest we should use psychic detectives or that we should take more time to research the matter."

For all that the attacks of CSICOP and similar organizations seem overly hostile, there is some basis for their outrage at the tricks used by pseudopsychics in the past.

Chapter Five

Pseudopsychic Tricks

WE RETURN TO THE QUESTION WE STARTED with: Do some people somehow know things other people don't?

Skeptics say no, and they offer several other explanations for what is seemingly a successful psychic consultation. The alternative explanation they most frequently offer is the various tricks of a "cold reading." This term originated with phony spiritualist mediums in the 1920s, and it describes how they dealt with a client who walked in off the street "cold"—in other words, a client about whom they knew nothing.

Phony mediums used psychological techniques to gather information from the client. Then they fed that information back to the client, who then often firmly believed that the information came from the psychic alone.

The fake mediums did this by leading the client to give them cues or by listening carefully to how the client interpreted what they said. If a medium said, for example, "You'll meet a tall, dark, attractive stranger," the client might blush and say, "Oh, do you mean Rebecca?" (Or Harold, as the case may be.) The medium then simply went on to talk to the client about his or her incipient relationship with Rebecca or Harold, and the client went willingly and naively along with the "reading."

The trickery wasn't always this obvious. Some charlatans became adept at reading incredibly subtle cues from the client's body language. They delivered bits of information, all the while watching the client for twitches, grimaces, changes of posture, and the like and allowing those reactions to guide them to their next "prediction."

Given enough practice, this isn't hard to do. Even many animals are extraordinarily good at reading cues because animals are almost naturally intuitive around people. Consider how your pet always seems to know when it's time to "get lost" or to snuggle close and offer friendship.

Some animals have even become famous because of their ability, like the horse Clever Hans, whose answers to questions that were seemingly impossible for an animal to understand—or care about—were communicated with a coded series of hoof movements. He was responding, like a sheepdog, to changes in his handler's posture, gestures, facial expression, and other cues.

Fishing for information was another trick used by phony mediums. "I see the letter *S*," the pseudopsychic might say. "Oh!" said the client, a little startled. "Shirley? Or—no, it's got to be Sharon! Two of my best friends are Sharon and Shirley!" "That's right," said the psychic, and usually later the client wouldn't recall the source of the information, thinking instead that the psychic came up with the name with no help.

The simplest way to work a cold reading was to have a stock spiel—some memorized lines that were highly general and could fit most people. The client listened and thought the statements applied specifically to him or her. Psychologists call this the Barnum effect, after circus owner P. T. Barnum, who said that a sucker was born every minute.

Anyone who reads the horoscope in the daily newspaper has read lots of stock spiel. For example, it is difficult to know what the statement "People continue to rely on you, but you need to pay attention to yourself today" means specifically. But it's awfully nice to hear not only that you're reliable but that you also deserve to be a little selfish today.

There is often some stock spiel in the pronouncements of psychic sleuths. Many readings for missing persons, for example, will lead the psychic to "see water." Later, if the missing person's body is found after authorities have dragged the bottom of the local river, the psychic can claim he or she was right. The same claim could be made if the body is found draped over a sump pump in a basement or in a rain-filled gutter. Pseudopsychics are skillfully vague and ambiguous, allowing their clients to read clarity into their fuzzy statements. Superficially specific predictions that are actually ambiguous can lead to "self-fulfilling prophecies."

Some phony psychics were also as good at observation and deduction as Sherlock Holmes was. A palm reader, for example, could examine the lines of a client's hand and at the same time check to see if the client was a nervous nail-biter or was vain enough to have the nails professionally manicured. Social psychologists call this "unobtrusive measurement."

Another ploy was shotgunning—throwing out so much general information that one or more bits of it would almost surely be on target. A client who had an overwhelming interest in the outcome of the session—the parent of a missing child, for example, or a close relative of a murder victim—couldn't help responding when a bit of information did hit. Even subtle reactions helped the "psychic" hone in on a likely path to follow up.

Playing a game of multiple endpoints gave psychics a way not only to get information from a client, but also a way out of making an incorrect statement. A classic example of this is illustrated by the following exchange:

Phony psychic: "I see from your hand that you're artistic."

Client: "Why, yes. I do paint a little. In fact, I'm a professional artist."

Phony psychic: "I thought so!"

But if the client reacted in a way that suggested the psychic was wrong, the psychic could simply add, "I don't mean that you paint or draw. I mean that you have taste."

Few people think they're absolutely tasteless, so the phony psychic was off the hook on that bit of information and could easily go on to the next bit.

These tricks are all means by which a pseudopsychic could imitate the real thing. But here's where it gets really tricky, because most *real* psychics also use these methods—and so do private detectives, police detectives, and librarians who help researchers find the question they're *really* asking for help with. Many professionals collect evidence, make assessments, ask questions, make informed guesses, and practice the art of deductive thinking just as phony psychics do.

As the authors of *The Blue Sense* point out, there's a lot in what the great criminologist and psychical researcher Cesare Lombroso once said: "Just because there are wigs does not mean there is no real hair." He meant that the presence of some unscrupulous charlatans doesn't mean that all psychics are phony.

Finally, no one—least of all a true psychic—should imagine that every reading is valid. In many criminal investigations, the necessity of sifting psychic information to take what is useful is just as important as accurately interpreting what remains. Many psychics will claim that they're 80-90 percent right. When pressed, most will adjust their statement to mean that they produced something helpful in that percentage of cases.

Dr. Louise Ludwig told the authors of *The Blue Sense* that a good psychic can hit an everyday 20-25 percent accuracy rate in specific predictions. On a good day, the accuracy rate rises to 40 percent. On the best day of a psychic's life, the accuracy rate can reach 80 percent. Guided by those accuracy rates, police must decide in any given case if the potential benefit of following up on psychic leads outweighs the potential cost.

As a private person, you can tell if a psychic is real or phony by using the same costs-versus-benefits evaluation and by exercising a bit of caution. Be suspicious if you're asked to keep coming back—one or two sessions should be enough to learn everything the psychic knows about a specific matter. Be suspicious if the psychic keeps asking for more money—a real psychic's fee is usually agreed upon in advance, with no additional charges. Be suspicious if a psychic keeps milking *you* for information. And, yes, you can ask for a psychic demonstration with information you can verify. You can ask for credentials, too. A real psychic will have names of clients he or she has worked with and will indicate that he or she has no problem with your checking with them.

Chapter Six
Modern Psychic Sleuths

Ever since there have been stories, there have been stories about how a ghost or a dream came to solve a crime.

In early tales, the source of information was outside the person who solved the crime. In today's tales, the most frequent source of information is within the person who "witnesses" the crime. The witness or "seer" is credited with a psychic gift that helps her or him resolve something that's baffled the authorities.

The history of modern psychic detection paralleled the development of psychical research in general, beginning in the late nineteenth century. Britain's Society for Psychical Research was founded in 1882, and the American Society for Psychical Research in 1885. The scientists in these societies were interested in investigating the phenomena claimed by those in the Spiritualist movement.

Modern Spiritualism started in 1847 when the

Fox sisters of Hydesville, New York, said they heard spirit rappings in their home. Kate and Margaret Fox sat at a table and asked questions of their visiting spirit, a being called Mr. Splitfoot. As scary as his name sounded, the spirit was helpful. He answered their questions by rapping once for *no,* twice for *yes,* and three times if the question couldn't be answered.

It didn't take long before news of this spread, and the Fox sisters were a national sensation. Soon there were many mediums across the country. When, in 1899, Margaret confessed that she had caused the rappings by cracking a joint of her big toe—a confession she later took back—that news didn't stop public interest.

The Fox sisters were also the first modern psychic detectives, and the criminal case they worked on had to do with the identity of their spirit. In 1848, the spirit rapped out information about himself in code. He was a thirty-one-year-old peddler who had unfortunately called at the Hydesville house in which the Fox sisters now lived. He'd been murdered for his money by someone whose initials were C. R., who then buried him in the cellar.

The cellar was dug up that summer, and human

hair, some bones, and part of a skull were found. The immediate suspect was a man named Charles B. Rosana, a previous tenant who had moved to Lyons, New York. Rosana said he was innocent and went so far as to acquire the signatures, on a petition, of forty-four people who swore to his good character.

That took care of the matter until 1904, when excavation of a wall in the Hydesville house uncovered most of the rest of the skeleton's bones, as well as a tin peddler's box. With that, the case seemed to be solved, but there were a lot of loose ends—just as there are in most criminal cases today's psychic sleuths claim to have solved.

The loose ends in this case gave the scientists in the psychical societies plenty to chew over and debate, just as did the alleged identification of the man behind one of the world's most famous—and earliest—serial killers, Jack the Ripper. London medium Robert James Lees's role in the Ripper case, in fact, continues to be hotly debated.

The Ripper murders began on August 7, 1888, when the first of his six (some argue there were as many as eight or nine) victims met death in the Whitechapel district of London's East End. At least five of the dead women were prostitutes, and all of them were horribly butchered. The last of the murders was committed on November 9, but the ten-week period during which the Ripper "worked" was a time of terror for Londoners.

The first reference tying Lees to the case came from the criminal himself, whoever he was. In a July 25, 1889, letter to Scotland Yard, the FBI of Great Britain, someone signing himself "Jack the Ripper" wrote: "Dear Boss, You have not caught me yet you see, with all your cunning, with all your 'Lees,' with all your blue bottles." "Blue bottles" referred to the pesky, flylike, blue-coated police.

Lees, a medium known for his alleged spirit photography and other phenomena, was also a journalist and author. He wrote several books on spiritualism. Queen Victoria is said to have given him royal patronage, and he was highly respected by everyone who knew him. Lees wasn't a publicity hound; he avoided being associated with anything unsavory, and his lifelong reputation was clean and unblemished.

At the height of the Ripper murders, Lees had a clairvoyant vision that disturbed him so much that he took it to Scotland Yard. The Yard dismissed him as a crackpot, but the next night's murder followed Lees's vision. Later, Lees had another vision of a murder, this time with the victim's ears being cut off. Again Lees took his information to the Yard, where he was taken a little more seriously after investigators learned that police had just gotten a card from the Ripper in which he wrote about cutting off the ears of his next victim. The story goes that when Lees's third vision, just before the last Ripper murder, took him to the Yard, it was so precise and accurate that the Yard took Lees to the scene of the crime.

From there, Lees led authorities straight to the door of a respected West End physician. Questioning the doctor's wife resulted in the information that the doctor had been away from home during the very times the murders were committed and that he suffered from brief periods of amnesia. The doctor also had a sort of split personality, being kind and gentle at some times but cruel and sadistic at others. Further investigation led twelve London doctors to certify the physician as insane, and he was secretly committed to a private asylum.

Although Lees afterward steadfastly refused to name this mad doctor, his description of the doctor and the doctor's home pointed to physician Sir William

Gull being the Ripper.

But not all "Ripperologists"—people who continue to debate the case—agree. Their arguments and
counterarguments sound a lot like today's media arguments about the role of current psychics in current
unsolved crimes.

One skeptic is Dr. Donald J. West, a criminologist and specialist in psychic research. Dr. West would
have it that the three major elements of the story—
Lees's correctness in "seeing" the cutoff ears, Lees's visits to the authorities and their recognizing and using his
powers, and the identity and fate of the mad doctor—
all lack adequate supporting evidence. West points out
that Lees, being a journalist, would have had prior
access to the information about the cutoff ears, since
that news was first received by the Central News
Agency. Also, a commissioner at the Yard denied Lees's
involvement entirely, saying that the Yard had no
records about the psychic at all. And, lastly, the
mad-doctor story is seemingly belied by the actions of
police after Gull's asylum committal: They continued
to arrest other suspects, which they wouldn't have done
if they were sure the Ripper had been safely put away.

Lees's defenders agree that Lees could have

known of the ear-cutting threat, but they point out that *could*-have-known doesn't mean *did*-know. They insist the psychic didn't know. Also, since Lees's story mentioned that a cover-up was involved, poor coordination of police efforts could explain both the Yard's denial of Lees's involvement and the later arrests.

Another skeptic is Melvin Harris, a writer and British Broadcasting Corporation researcher. Harris compares Lees's own version of events, which became available only after he died, and his diary with the actual chronology of events. There are deviations.

To these arguments, Lees's defenders say that Lees's version of the events was written decades after the events and that failing memory accounts for his errors in details. Also, they argue, there's some evidence that Lees's diary may have been altered later. They point to the Ripper's letter of July 25, 1889, to support their position and also to a June 1987 interview a relative of Sir William Gull gave to writer Peter Underwood. In this interview, the relative told Underwood that "according to a family legend" he was a descendant of Jack the Ripper.

Sir Arthur Conan Doyle, who created Sherlock Holmes, was a staunch member of the British Society for Psychical Research. His own feeling was that the Ripper was a woman, but he was sufficiently scientific to write to Lees on November 6, 1928, to urge Lees to write about his psychic experiences in the case in order "to leave a clear record behind." Lees did so, noting that what he wrote should not be opened until 1931. When it was opened after Lees's death, the news about his visions and Sir William Gull became public knowledge—and fuel for continued debate.

Conan Doyle also got involved in the mysterious disappearance of another famous mystery writer—Agatha Christie. In 1926, when police found Christie's car, with its engine still running, on the edge of a chalk pit and suspected foul play, Conan Doyle got in touch with a medium who specialized in accurate psychometric readings. The results of that reading appeared in a letter Conan Doyle wrote to the *Morning Post:*

> In this case, I obtained a glove of Mrs. Christie's, and asked an excellent psychometrist for an opinion. I gave him no clue at all as to what I wanted or to whom the article belonged. He never saw it until I laid it on the table at the moment of

consultation, and there was nothing to connect either it or me with the Christie case. The date was Sunday last. He at once got the name of Agatha. "There is trouble connected with this article. The person who owns it is half dazed and half purposeful. She is not dead as many think. She is alive. You will hear of her, I think, next Wednesday."

Mrs. Christie was found on Tuesday night, but it was actually Wednesday when the news reached us, so everything in the reading, so far as I could test it . . . proved to be true. The only error was that he had an impression of water, though whether the idea of a Hydro [a spa] was at the bottom of this feeling is at least arguable. I sent the report on to Colonel Christie that evening.

Agatha Christie had been found at a hotel spa in northern England, registered under the name of the woman her husband had told her he wanted to marry. She said she suffered from amnesia, a loss of memory.

The history of modern psychic sleuths includes teenagers like Eugenie Dennis, who frequently got full public credit from police for her efforts in investigations. Gene Dennis was born in Atchison, Kansas, where her high-school fame in finding lost objects brought her to the attention of David P. Abbott. Abbott had made a name for himself exposing fake mediums, ultimately writing the debunking classic *Behind the Scenes with the Mediums.* He tested Gene for four weeks and ended by declaring that she had a "God-given ability."

Two years after their meeting, in 1922, when Dennis was sixteen, Abbott became her manager and set up a tour for her through the western states, which was highly successful. Her stage performances consisted of simply standing onstage and answering questions put to her by members of the audience.

Dennis offered her services to police departments in many cities on her tour. They gave her minor cases at first: She found fifteen stolen bicycles in Joplin, Missouri; she found a parole violator in St. Louis for the police department in Chillicothe, Missouri; she found twenty-three missing diamonds in Omaha, Nebraska. She also signed a three-year movie deal with a Kansas film production company.

The next year, when she was seventeen, the stakes in her cases went up. Dennis found stolen jewels valued at several hundred thousand dollars in New York City.

A month later, in March, a Mrs. Mary Foley brought charges against Gene and her mother for fortune-telling. A couple of prominent skeptics—Hereward Carrington and Harry Houdini, the magician—surprised the court when they appeared to testify in Dennis's favor.

During a 1934 tour of England, Dennis became involved with a sensational case, the "No. 1 Brighton Trunk crime." On July 17, a luggage clerk at the Brighton railway station discovered a trunk containing a human torso. The trunk had been left in the cloakroom eleven days earlier. Although Dennis didn't solve this crime, she did give police information about the victim that was later confirmed by renowned pathologist Sir Bernard Spilsbury. She also predicted that another, similar crime would come to light. A few weeks later, a house-to-house search by police uncovered a second trunk containing another torso in a locked and empty lodging house.

The next ten years found Gene Dennis performing less and less often in public, while her private clientele grew. At only forty-one, she died in Seattle, Washington, on March 8, 1948.

Plump, warmhearted grandmothers have also won fame as psychic sleuths. Mrs. Florence Sternfels, known publicly simply as Florence, worked at about the same time as Gene Dennis. Florence "has probably read more people and solved more crimes, in cooperation with the police, than any medium who ever lived," said a member of the American Psychical Institute. From her storybook house overlooking the Hudson River in small Edgewater, New Jersey, Florence gave public readings in her home for which she charged one dollar. She also worked with police, without pay, for more than forty years.

She was helpful and beloved. Edgewater police chief Edward Pickering said that Florence's help had been sought not only by agencies in the United States but from foreign countries—England's Scotland Yard and France's Sûreté. Florence herself mentioned solving thefts for insurance companies and private investigators. Captain John Cronin of New York's Missing Persons Bureau said, "I've known Florence twenty-five years. She's right seventy-five percent of the time."

She impressed the manager of the Bell Telephone Company so deeply when she told him where he'd misplaced some important papers that he allowed her to be listed in the Manhattan and New Jersey telephone directories simply as "Florence, Psychic."

Apart from her directory listing, Florence made little effort to promote herself. The sign on the door of her home, left standing open, read FLORENCE, PSYCHOMETRIST. WALK IN. And people did walk in, from the time she began her workday at 8:00 P.M. until she closed the door, sometimes as late as 2:00 A.M.

She claimed to be neither a fortune-teller nor a spiritualist. "In fact, if I ever saw a real ghost, I think I'd faint from sheer fright," she said.

Her cases ran a gamut from missing objects to missing persons and from murder to wartime national security. Sometimes she had to deal with people she didn't like. One of these was Dutch Schultz, a notorious New York gangster. Schultz came to see Florence on October 21, 1935, and she told him two things. First, she said she didn't like his manner, and second, she said Schultz should stay out of Newark, New Jersey. Schultz didn't. Two days later, Florence read the front-page news of his death, in the back room of a Newark bar.

But if there were well-known psychics who "weren't into tricks" like Gene Dennis and Florence, there were also famed psychics like Peter Hurkos, who were, if not into tricks, at least into slippery self-promotion.

Hurkos, an immigrant from Greece, claimed that his psychic powers came to him after he fell thirty feet from a ladder while painting a building and landed on his head and shoulder. From then on, Hurkos's life seemed to be either feast or famine, pain or plenty. He rode a roller-coaster of prosperity and poverty that seemed to be entirely of his own making, although he blamed other people when things weren't going well.

His most publicized case came to him during one of the "valleys" of his life. He was in Beverly Hills staying in the home of his friend and patron, actor Glenn Ford, awaiting the completion of his second divorce, when he was invited to participate in the investigation of the Boston Strangler.

That case had started on June 14, 1962, when Mrs. Anna Slesers was raped and killed in her Boston apartment. Ten more women were sexually assaulted and strangled over the next eighteen months. The citizens of Boston were growing increasingly fearful, and a concerned industrialist offered a deal to Assistant Attorney General John Bottomly, who was in charge of coordinating the search for the Strangler. The industrialist said he and some friends of his would foot the bill if Bottomly would get Hurkos in on the case. Bottomly agreed, bringing Hurkos in on January 29, 1964.

Bottomly later said that he didn't worry about whether Hurkos was psychic or not. Even if Hurkos wasn't psychic, he would be useful because he would bring a fresh approach to the investigation. That approach would have the added value of being one seasoned by previous work in bizarre and difficult cases like the one at hand. In fact, if Hurkos's efforts served only to irritate Boston's detectives, it would be good, Bottomly said. Irritation would make the Boston detectives work even harder, to prove that Hurkos was a fake, and their increased efforts could be advantageous to solving the crimes.

Although Bottomly's statements sound deeply cynical, his stance was one that is often adopted by police who call in psychics. Information from psychic sleuths, even if false, can trigger an officer's thinking into fresh, and more productive, avenues. Or it can serve police well as a way to "launder" their own information through the media and thus force a suspect's hand without themselves getting caught in a legal trap that could destroy a case in court. In addition, police can "leak" information they want to get out by using psychics. They can also use psychic information to restart an investigation their superiors may have stopped due to a lack of evidence.

No matter why Hurkos was involved in the Boston Strangler case, that he was involved in it from the moment he and his bodyguard got to town goes without saying. Hurkos impressed Bottomly and others working on the case with a show of information he "saw" about them. And when a police sergeant handed Hurkos a letter to examine, it appeared the case was closed. "My God, son of a bitch, he do it!" Hurkos declared in his broken English, sitting bolt upright. "This is the one—he's the murderer!"

The letter was from a shoe salesman looking for a wife. He had written to the Boston College of Nursing to ask for a list of its students. Police talked to the salesman, found him to be psychotic and paranoid, and had him committed for tests and further investigation. They took Hurkos to the mental hospital to interview the salesman, and later that evening Hurkos said,

"My work finished." He prepared to leave Boston for New York.

Days later, Hurkos was roused from sleep in his hotel room and arrested by the FBI. He was taken to jail and held for nine hours, until Dr. Puharich, who had conducted years of tests to determine Hurkos's psychic abilities, bailed him out. The charges were that in the previous year, while driving across country with the aim of looking into the kidnapping of Frank Sinatra, Jr., Hurkos had led people in a Milwaukee gas station to believe that he was an FBI agent. Hurkos said it was all a mistake caused by his bad English. He'd been showing off some of his honorary police badges when someone asked if he was FBI. Hurkos replied that he was *more* than that.

In the end, the judge believed Hurkos's story, but before the psychic went to trial, the press had a heyday. HURKOS FRAMED, one paper's headline read. Another paper mockingly countered with the headline PSYCHIC SLEUTH FAILED TO SEE FBI ON HIS TRAIL. A furious Bottomly saw the whole affair as an attempt to discredit not only Hurkos but also himself and his staff.

In the midst of all this wrangling, the Boston Strangler investigation continued to grind along. Before the year was over, Albert DeSalvo confessed to being the Strangler. Hurkos went on insisting that the salesman was the real killer, but the weight of both public opinion and the evidence was clearly against him.

And his arrest caused other problems in Hurkos's life. It stopped plans for a movie based on his life, and his Hollywood friends deserted him. To replace what he'd lost, Hurkos took to the bottle. But all this despair led to another peak in his life. Hurkos met the woman who would become his third wife, as well as an aggressive new business manager, and his career took off again.

In 1968 Hurkos played himself in a film about the Boston Strangler, and in 1969 he was earning $2,500 for a weekend at a Lake Tahoe nightclub and $10,000 for a week at a Los Angeles theater.

All in all, the Boston Strangler case and later episodes in Hurkos's life have led serious psychic investigators to call him a "psychic scoundrel."

Can the debate about the reality of psychic powers, let alone their usefulness in criminal investigations, ever be resolved? Some experts think it can and *must* be, and they have some ideas on how to help do that.

Chapter Seven
Toward a New Investigative Team

THE UNITED STATES DEPARTMENT OF JUSTICE'S *Report to the Nation on Crime and Justice* of March 1988 predicted that at current crime rates, almost everyone will be a victim of some kind of crime in his or her lifetime.

That's unhappy news. Even more unhappy is the news that the percentage of crimes solved by arrest hasn't gone up since the 1970s. In fact, the arrest percentage has decreased in some heavily urbanized areas.

These facts, combined with heavy media coverage of stories dealing with drugs, child molestation, rape, and murder, have led to growing public anxiety. The "thin blue line" of law enforcement officers seems to be stretched to the point of snapping, and many people wonder if local and federal police agencies can fulfill their mission to serve and protect.

As in any time when the world appears to be going out of control, when expectations of "normal" things happening are frustrated time and again, people turn to "abnormal" means to regulate their lives. These days, as far as criminal investigations are concerned, those abnormal means often are "paranormal" means.

And so even with the dread of the "giggle factor" in the backs of their minds should they use a psychic and still fail to solve a crime, more and more police agencies are seriously considering the use of psychic information as an investigative aid, and many police departments are already using such information in this way.

And so a psychic like Dixie Yeterian of Alaska paces over the actual crime scene and passes along to police the information she receives. Or a psychic like Nancy Czetli visits the place or pours over videotapes of the crime scene, linking her mind with the victim's while feeling as if she's standing alongside him or her. Other psychics say they need only a typographical map of the area. Still others want a photograph and a name. Many like to handle an object that's been in close proximity to either the victim or the suspect and "read" that psychometrically.

Psychics Greta Alexander and Noreen Renier prefer to work at long distance, over the telephone.

Alexander says she gained her psychic abilities after being struck by lightning. She then had a vision of the Virgin Mary and began hearing "angels" talk to her. Renier simply switches over to the right side of her brain.

The method of psychic Marinus Dykshoorn is to go over a crime scene with a loop of piano wire, which he uses like an antenna to pick up vibrations of what happened there. Father-and-daughter psychics Louis and Ginette Mattacia dowse for criminals, just as their seventeenth-century counterparts did. Bill Ward and Dorothy Allison use astrology along with experiencing events from the criminal's point of view.

Psychic John Catchings of Texas has achieved a national reputation for his specialty—finding dead bodies. Another psychic, Kathlyn Rhea of Cupertino, California, also has a reputation for finding bodies. Greta Alexander says she has more luck locating drowning victims than others. Psychic Phil Jordan has had documented success in his specialty, which is the finding of *live* bodies—missing persons.

Missing animals are also the focus of psychic searches. Pat Huff, who operates the Parapsychology Center of Toledo, Ohio, found some stolen pedigree

Persian show cats in 1989. The specialty of Hollywood psychic Beatrice Lydecker is "talking" to animals. In 1978 she was instrumental in saving the life of a German shepherd accused of eating parts of his master, who had been killed in an auto crash. The dog was condemned to death, but the real culprits were coyotes and wild dogs, the traumatized dog told Lydecker. He was spared, which makes at least one happy ending in the oftentimes grisly world of criminology.

Some psychics specialize in finding treasure. Ron Warmouth of Los Angeles works on criminal cases and dowses for oil and gas on the side. Ingo Swann, who became famous for remote viewing (visualizing places many miles away) in the 1970s, has also earned corporate dollars hunting for oil. Israeli Uri Geller reportedly made a fortune in the early 1980s pinpointing oil and mineral deposits for mining and drilling corporations and now runs his own company in London with the help of engineers and geologists. Most psychics, however, respond to the emotions typically exhibited in violent crimes—terror and hate—rather than to rocks.

In addition to growing numbers of professional psychics with special areas of expertise, there are now landmark judicial decisions that support the use of their abilities. One significant case in 1978 involved the collaboration of a psychic named "Joan" with Los Angeles police artist Fernando Ponce.

After five days of investigation that turned up no leads in the disappearance of seven-year-old Carl Carter, Jr., of South Gate, California, detectives contacted Joan. She immediately told them that the boy had been murdered by a man who had killed before. The police artist made a composite sketch of the killer from Joan's impressions. When the sketch was shown to the missing boy's parents, they both said it looked like Harold Ray "Butch" Memro, a thirty-three-year-old boat-company worker who was an acquaintance of the family. Police questioned Memro, who was on probation for child molestation. On the basis of his record and his remarks, Memro was arrested. He confessed to the Carter murder as well as to the unsolved murders of two other young boys two years earlier.

At the trial, Memro's attorneys attacked the legal basis of the arrest on the grounds of probable cause. The arrest, they said, had grown out of the psychic reading. But Los Angeles Superior Court judge William McGinley ruled that the use of the psychic in the case was merely an "investigative tool . . . that may be used to follow up additional leads.

The police dread of the "giggle factor" and its leading to failure was clearly soothed in Judge McGinley's ruling. And the world of science is adding more support to the validity of paranormal knowledge. (The "giggle factor" could have been lessened by the ruling, but it was the dread that was soothed.)

Relativity, recent developments in quantum mechanics, and theories in physics about alternative and parallel universes have turned traditional materialistic science upside down. Some physicists are persuaded that psychic abilities and knowledge are not only possible but probable.

The work of two scientists in particular might explain how the work of psychic sleuths aligns with growing realizations about the nature of time. These scientists are Professor Robert G. Jahn, now director of the Engineering Anomalies Research Project at Princeton University, and Dr. Edwin C. May, who headed psychic research at SRI International. They are primarily interested in precognition—that is, the knowledge of events before they have happened. Perhaps some of their insights will explain the retrocognition of psychics, who see events like crimes as they happened in the past.

Other parapsychologists are simply attempting to find a useful application for psi, the force behind psychic abilities. They are working with applied parapsychology, what some of its proponents call psionics. The basis of their work is that an idea (or phenomenon) gains scientific acceptance if a sufficiently practical use for it exists, as has happened often in the history of science. Acceptance comes even if no one understands in theory why something works the way it does.

One example of this is anesthesia in medicine. Why and how an anesthetic works is still largely a physiological mystery, but it's one mystery never questioned by anyone going into surgery!

If it can be proven that psychics can solve crimes, no one will argue with the process, and some brilliant scientist may even be given access to the funds and time needed to discover how it all works.

Already, as we have seen, there are psychics who pragmatically hunt for oil. There are others who predict the ratings of a particular TV show or "read" the stock market for private clients.

Few parapsychologists have studied the uses of psi in criminology, although at least one group of behavioral scientists has looked at the issue from another vantage point. PsiCom, mentioned earlier, had as its main goal not to understand how psychic sleuths worked, but instead to help police departments develop their own psychics within the force. They attempted to train police officers to be less analytical and more intuitive—in other words, less left-brained and more right-brained.

As things stand now, the words of a psychic are not probable cause for a search warrant, and the "knowings" of a psychic are usually not admissible as evidence in court. In this, psychic information is like the results of most lie detector tests, information gained from someone who has been given truth serums, and even sometimes identification of suspects through DNA sampling or "genetic fingerprinting."

But psychic information is now indirectly used in court anyway. Not only does psychic information guide many police investigations, but some attorneys have also turned to psychics for help in jury selection.

Some researchers in parapsychology believe that by the end of the century, not only will the reality of psi be indisputably proven, but also that a cadre of reliable psychics will have been trained to work in law enforcement, national security, and defense.

As long ago as 1928, Chief Justice Louis D. Brandeis wrote a dissenting opinion in *Olmstead v. United States,* a wiretap case. He said, "The progress of science in furnishing the government with means of espionage is not likely to stop with wiretapping. Ways may someday be developed by which the government, without removing papers from secret drawers, can reproduce them in court, and by which it will be enabled to expose to a jury the most intimate occurrences of the home. Advances in the psychic and related sciences may bring means of exploring unexpressed beliefs, thoughts and emotions."

That shouldn't sound scary to those of us who will be victims of one crime or another if current crime rates hold steady. Victims of crimes, according to United States Department of Justice projections, will be all of us—directly. So all of us will benefit if crime is deterred by whatever means, including the use of psychic sleuths.

But if the situation Chief Justice Brandeis described were to happen, then we all would certainly need to reassess many features of life that most of us currently say we believe in—features like, for example, our constitutional right to privacy.

The same complexity operates when we think of a new kind of criminal investigative team that would openly and as a matter of course include psychics.

On the one side, some skeptics worry about bringing "medieval justice" into the modern courtroom. They paint a frightening picture of unreliable psychics accusing anybody they wish of anything they wish, a picture that brings to mind the Salem witch trials. They want justice based on scientific evidence, although they are often oddly opposed to any means of regulating psychics to aid in the gathering of evidence.

The authors of *The Blue Sense* report a different attitude in the psychics they spoke with in their research. They found that many psychics felt the need for organization, if for no other reason than to be able to refer police in other countries or states to competent colleagues. They expressed concern about the bad apples working in their field, as well as a hope that there might be licensing for their work in the future so that ethical standards could be created and maintained.

When considering these complexities, it is well to remember some facts: One is that justice is, by its very nature, *not* a scientific goal. It is a human goal.

Another is that criminal investigation remains more an art than a science. Even when the seeming "magic" of nuclear-age scientific advances is applied to the field of criminology, that knowledge is applied by all-too-human humans.

For Further Reading

Archer, Fred. *Crime and the Psychic World.* New York: William Morrow and Company, Inc., 1969.

Duncan, Lois. *Don't Look Behind You.* New York: Delacorte, 1989.

———. *Who Killed My Daughter? The True Story of a Mother's Search for Her Daughter's Murderer.* New York: Delacorte, 1992.

Gardner, Robert. *Crime Lab 101.* New York: Walker and Company, 1992.

Gustafson, Anita. *Guilty or Innocent?* New York: Holt, 1985.

Larsen, Anita. *Lost . . . and Never Found.* New York: Scholastic, 1984.

———. *Lost . . . and Never Found II.* New York: Scholastic, 1991.

———. *True Crimes and How They Were Solved.* New York: Scholastic, 1993.

Lyons, Arthur, and Marcello Truzzi. *The Blue Sense.* New York: The Mysterious Press, 1991.

Index

 ## About the Author

Anita Larsen is the author of numerous books for young readers. She lives with her dog, Amelie, in New Mexico.

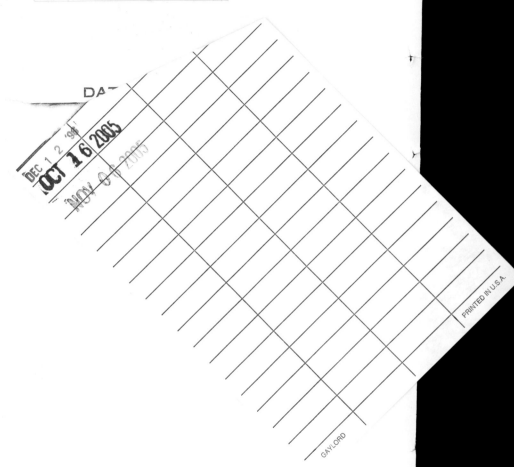